POSTCARD HISTORY SERIES

Fort Campbell

IN VINTAGE POSTCARDS

Save

Souvenir BASEBALL *Program*

Camp Campbell Post Team

CAMP CAMPBELL, KY.

Season of 1943

The 12th Armored Division baseball team played an 11-game schedule in 1943. This program was for the game with the 20th Armored Division. The camp commander at the time was calvary colonel Guy W. Chipman. The team manager was Cpl. Jimmie Reese, Division Service Company, and the team director was Maj. Lester D. Friend, Camp Campbell special service officer. The program contains the names of players from both teams.

POSTCARD HISTORY SERIES

Fort Campbell

IN VINTAGE POSTCARDS

Billyfrank Morrison

Published by Arcadia Publishing
Charleston SC, Chicago IL, Portsmouth NH, San Francisco CA

Printed in Great Britain

Library of Congress Catalog Card Number: 2005925646

For all general information contact Arcadia Publishing at:
Telephone 843-853-2070
Fax 843-853-0044
E-mail sales@arcadiapublishing.com
For customer service and orders:
Toll-Free 1-888-313-2665

Visit us on the internet at http://www.arcadiapublishing.com

The Screaming Eagles of the 327th are shown as they pass in review on a gamma goat. The tower in the background indicates this event took place on Campbell Army Air Field (CAAF) tarmac. A number of people are observing from the catwalk of the old air control tower. The tower and the chimney seen in back have since been demolished.

CONTENTS

ACKNOWLEDGMENTS

Those who provided assistance and information are too numerous to name, but without them the book would have been lacking. Much of what is contained in the book is the result of historical research. Much of it was derived from personal interviews with soldiers and civilian employees of Fort Campbell, some still actively involved in the operation of the post and others retired.

I would also like to pay tribute to a great friend of the Fort Campbell community who passed away while I was working on the book. Carlton Walker Bousman Sr., owner and operator of Gate Three Printing, was one of Fort Campbell's most enthusiastic devotees. I stopped and talked with Carlton shortly before his death. We talked, of course, about Fort Campbell. Carlton was an army veteran who never forgot the army or Fort Campbell. It is only fitting that he be mentioned here. And last, but certainly not least, thank you to the Fort Campbell soldiers who have served our country and been put "in harm's way." I would especially like to recognize the Fort Campbell soldiers who have lost their lives in Iraq while I was compiling the book.

The 101st honor guard, in dress blue uniforms, participates in a flag ceremony. The flag being dipped is the division headquarters standard.

INTRODUCTION

Let me say immediately that a book of this volume can in no way encompass even a small part of what Fort Campbell means to this country. In the book, I offer some information about Fort Campbell that strikes me as being important and some information that is unimportant but interesting. The book contains both positive and unfortunate information about the post and its soldiers.

Collecting Fort Campbell postcards started while I was teaching at Fort Campbell High School many years ago. The collecting continued as I worked at CAAF the next few years. It became a passion between 1985 and 1994, during my work with the Installation Safety Office. The pleasure I find in collecting postcards has not diminished, and once again, I am working at Fort Campbell. These cards are pieces of evidence—some treasured—of the history of Fort Campbell and the heritage belonging to the soldiers who served there.

While there is a sequence to this book—it has contents and chapters—it is really a myriad of postcards, photographs, and stories about Fort Campbell soldiers and their "home away from home." Many readers will know or have heard the stories. Others will have personally been involved in them.

The author's cards have been showcased in *Tennessee Magazine*; on TV's "Tennessee Crossroads"; on Hopkinsville, Kentucky, television station WKAG; in a number of other books; and in the Clarksville, Tennessee, *Leaf Chronicle*. This book with its postcards will provide collectors, historians, and Fort Campbell soldiers past, present, and future an interesting look at the history they are an integral part of.

So go ahead—take a postcard tour of Camp and Fort Campbell, Kentucky.

Much has changed since the creation of Camp Campbell, but this building has changed very little and is easily recognized by all who visit the proud old post.

One

Welcome to Camp/Fort Campbell, Kentucky

Camp Campbell, Tennessee, was named in honor of Brig. Gen. William Bowen Campbell, once a colonel of the Bloody First Tennessee Volunteers. The camp was later re-designated Camp Campbell, Kentucky. In 1950, it became a permanent post and was named Fort Campbell, Kentucky. This "large letter" postcard contains a small image of Camp Campbell in each of the letters (the "M in Camp" is a picture of the interior of Service Club No. 2).

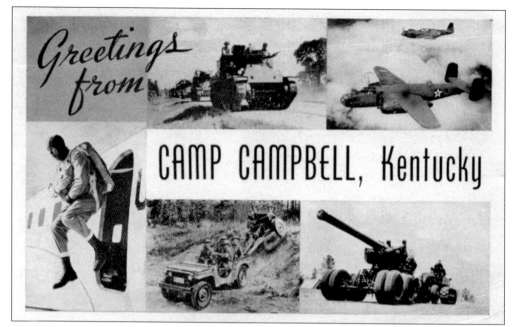

Clockwise from the left are a paratrooper exiting a C-47, a convoy of antiquated tanks, a U.S. Air Force Mustang and B-25, a "big gun" followed by a half-tracked vehicle, and an M-151 with an artillery piece in tow. This card was sent by "Elmira" to her "folks" in New Ulm, Minnesota, and states, "I'll go to the camp again today. He didn't come in last night. These long walks sure roll around fast."

In the summer of 1942, the initial cadre (20 strong) arrived from Fort Knox. During World War II, the 12th, 14th, and 20th Armored Divisions, Head Quarters (HQ) IV Armored Corps, and 26th Infantry Division were at Campbell. The 8th Armored Division (Thundering Herd) trained at Camp Campbell in 1943 and 1944, and during a short 63 days in World War II, the 8th Armored Division lost 260 killed and 1,015 wounded while capturing 35,000 POWs.

The 101st Airborne Division, which activated August 16, 1942, at Camp Claiborne, Louisiana, under Gen. William C. Lee, would make Fort Campbell its home. This sign shows it has been home to many commands. Three soldiers in BDUs (battle-dress uniforms) can be seen returning from Jewel Brick's Men's Store. Jewel was a Clarksvillian married to Gen. William H. Birdsong Jr., who retired while commanding general (CG) in 1972. Birdsong formed the 101 Club in 1973.

Clockwise from the top left are a rifle squad training, an unidentified patch, tanks being washed after tactical operations, troops disembarking from a CH-47, bazooka training, and presentation of colors. Some of these views can also be found on individual cards. Narrative on the back of the cards locates the post "57 miles NW of Nashville, 7 miles N of Clarksville, and 15 miles S of Hopkinsville, KY."

This card was printed in the mid–1960s and shows, clockwise from the top left, Post HQ, a Third Army patch, the new post chapel, the administrative building for the old hospital, paratroopers, and a U.S. Air Force C-124.

This linen postcard shows the HQ for the 12th Armored Division assigned to Camp Campbell during World War II. One unit in the 12th was the 152nd Armored Signal Company, which was activated here in September 1942. Today, everything but the HQ building has changed. All post decisions are made from here, including the one to name Fort Campbell High School sports teams for General Pratt's glider, the "Fighting Falcon."

Screaming Eagles

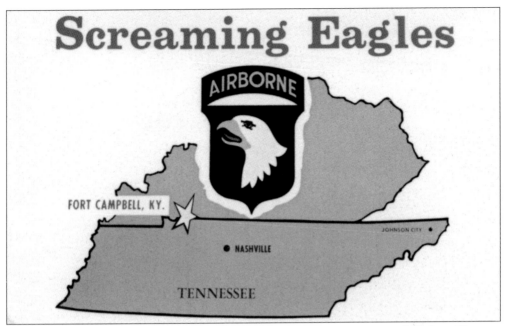

The back of this card states, "The Screaming Eagles returned to Fort Campbell from Vietnam in 1972." The date was April 6, and they were welcomed back by Vice Pres. Spiro Agnew and army Chief of Staff William C. Westmoreland. In the upper right-hand corner of the Tennessee outline is Johnson City. Why Johnson City, of all Tennessee cities, is shown is a mystery.

Camp Breckinridge at Morganfield, Kentucky, was home to the 101st Airborne Division during the early 1950s. The Screaming Eagle could be found on the two stone gates at the main entrance. The U.S. Army Signal Corps printed this and other cards of Camp Breckenridge.

Fort Campbell is a sprawling post that serves as home to the 101st and other major tenant units, such as 5th Special Forces Group (Airborne); 160th Special Operations Aviation Regiment (Airborne); U.S. Army Medical Activity, Tennessee Valley District; Veterinary Command; and U.S. Dental Activity. There are a number of smaller tenant units such as the 902nd Military Intelligence Group.

Lee Greenwood had plenty of help singing "I'm Proud to be an American." The adults standing are, from left to right, Forces Command (FORSCOM) commander Gen. Edwin Burka; Greenwood; the CG's wife, Pam Peay; Mrs. Barbara Bush; Col. John Seymour, garrison commander; and Seymour's wife, Mary. The Seymours divorced years ago. Mary has remarried and is still employed at Fort Campbell.

14

This is a post signal photograph of a somewhat humorous moment at CAAF. The soldier in the wig is unidentified (and is probably happy about that). According to unit historian Capt. Jim Page, the officer in the middle is Maxwell Davenport Taylor (1901–1987). Taylor commanded the 101st, was chairman of the Joint Chiefs of Staff, and served as ambassador to South Vietnam from 1964 to 1965, after Kennedy called him out of retirement.

In this photograph, the CG's secretary, Marie Warren, is presenting Colonel Honeycutt a Kentucky Colonel certificate. Marie was the command secretary for many years. Opportunists sold the numerous items of military ephemera that Marie collected throughout her career (including this photograph) after her death. Mrs. Warren was a wonderful person and remarkable civil servant.

A youthful Col. Colin Powell visits with Maj. Gen. John Brandenburg. Powell was injured in a helicopter crash in Vietnam, commanded the 2nd Brigade at Fort Campbell in 1976, and, under Pres. George W. Bush, was the first African American secretary of state. Col. Jim Hallums was Powell's S-1 and is most remembered for a sex scandal at West Point. Brandenburg was from New Hampshire and the only ROTC student to ever become a four-star general.

Fort Campbell troops pass in review at a change-of-command ceremony. A senior NCO (non-commissioned officer) said this photograph was taken when they still "marched in step." The grandstands are still here but are now covered to protect viewers from the elements.

Maj. Gen. Ben Sternberg was CG in 1966–1967 and is shown here presenting an award to Mrs. Warren.

Maj. Gen. George Hatton Weems (1891–1957), founder of Weems Academy in Clarksville, was a longtime friend of the Fort Campbell community, as was his brother Phillip Van Horn Weems (1889–1979). Phillip invented numerous navigational systems used today by commercial airlines, NASA, and aviation units at Fort Campbell; was an All-American football player and an Olympic wrestler; and was friends with both Charles Lindbergh and Orville Wright.

The world's only air assault division, the 101st has some of the most powerful and called-upon defense forces. It first earned its prestige during World War II in Bastogne, and the legacy continues. Mary Kohler, chief of protocol at Fort Campbell, identified the five soldiers up front. They are, from left to right, Brig. Gen. Edward Sinclair; Col. Thomas Schoenbeck; Richard Cody; Col. Kim Summers, garrison commander; and CSM Marvin Hill.

Vice President Bush is greeted by Maj. Gen. John Miller and his wife, Joan, at CAAF. Bush would become president, and Miller would become a lieutenant general. The vice president's father also visited Fort Campbell, as did Presidents Reagan and Johnson. While at Fort Campbell, Bush asked about the blue berets the 101st once wore to distinguish them from their rivals the 82nd, who wore red berets.

This wide-angle view gives some idea of the enormity of Fort Campbell. The post has an airfield capable of accommodating "anything that flies," more than 50 firing ranges, 5 drop zones, an assault air strip, 3 impact areas, a demolition area, 48 maneuver areas, 340 artillery firing points, and numerous other training areas.

Under Westmoreland's command in Vietnam from 1964 to 1968, the 101st featured large "search and destroy" sweeps. During this time, he repeatedly requested additional troops and got them. The 101st was in Vietnam more than four years. Westmoreland (shown here on the left) was the army Chief of Staff from 1968 to 1972. The general officer with him is unidentified.

426th FORWARD SUPPORT BATTALION

TO THE TASK

Fort Campbell, Kentucky

On June 23, 1993, the 426th Battalion (Forward) transferred command from Lt. Col. Peter B. Mack to Lt. Col. Richard T. Bierie at the Division Parade Field. In the event of inclement weather, the ceremony would be moved to Olive Physical Fitness Center. Gate Three Printing's Carlton Bousman and Bill Maki printed announcements for units on post for more than 20 years.

This card contains General Orders Number 179 of February 1, 1974, signed by Maj. Gen. Sidney Berry. It authorized the wearing of the Airmobile Badge by those who earned it.

Two

AVIATION

OH-6 Cayuses flew out of CAAF and other nearby locations around 1990—though at the time, the 160th denied that. The message on the card states, "The 160th would load these (in various colors) onto C-5 Galaxies or C-141s to fly to Central and South America." It was rare to see these at the time and rarer to find a photograph or postcard of them. The card refers to "6 to 12 160th aircraft at the bottom of Kentucky Lake."

Airborne units spearhead attacks, 1944

© USPS 1994

This is a Waco CG-4A glider, often called a flying coffin. Famed stunt pilot Hap Arnold was in the seat beside Brig. Gen. Don R. Pratt in one of the division's 52 gliders when a jeep broke loose on landing, and Pratt became only the second general officer to die in the war. As artillery fired in the background, Pratt was wrapped in a parachute and buried in a pasture. After the war, he was moved to Arlington National Cemetery.

The Taylorcraft L-2M Grasshopper was an early army fixed-wing aircraft that flew in and out of CAAF. During World War II, it was used in much the same manner as the World War I observation balloon, spotting enemy troops and supply concentrations and directing artillery fire on them. It was also used for liaison and light transport duties.

On April 23, 1958, just three weeks after Westmoreland (the youngest general in the army) assumed command of the 101st, he ordered a mass jump of 1,400 soldiers—in spite of winds that were marginally safe. The paratroopers landed on Highway 41 and beyond, resulting in five being dragged to death and 150 injured (including the young general, who jumped last). Today's chutes are equipped with a quick-release harness.

Troopers Ready for the Jump
Fort Campbell, Ky.

This 1950s postcard shows students of the Airborne Division Parachute School, Fort Campbell, as they assume the "get ready" position. Lucky Long got that name when a chute failed to open and he landed on the open canopy of another jumper. With the old T-10 chute, lines came out first, then silk—it was "one thousand, two thousand, whop!" Before the T-10, the tight-fitting harness was most uncomfortable.

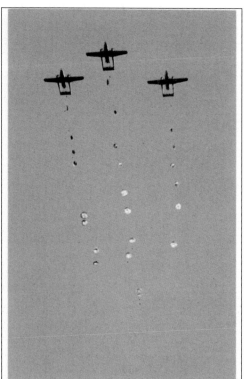

Three C-119s unload their cargo of troopers, all highly trained in airborne attack. A problem with the T-10 was that if wet, the silk stuck together and did not deploy well. This prevented jumps during rain. In Corrigidor, the 101st jumped from altitudes of 200 feet. Doing so rendered reserve chutes ineffective, as you would be on the ground before you could count to four seconds.

Mass Jump, Fort Campbell, Kentucky

U. S. ARMY PHOTO   1C-N620

This mass jump from C-119s is indicative of what the skies looked like during Operation Market Garden in Holland during World War II. The two U.S. Airborne divisions were under the command of Lt. Gen. Lewis Brereton. A paratrooper could be court marshaled if he got white smoke and a green light and did not exit the aircraft. Between 1942 and 1946, the 277th Parachute Field Artillery Battalion parachuted artillery pieces near the front lines.

The significance of this card is the mention (in narrative on the back of the card) of Clarksville Base. The base is referred to as "the Bird Cage" because the wrought-iron container in which the atomic weapon fusing device was secured and moved resembled a birdcage. If Debbie McGaha Bratton's efforts to write a book about Clarksville Base are not thwarted, it will provide some lights on phenomena about the secretive location.

This linen card shows a jump on Sukchon Drop Zone at Fort Campbell. Famed for the pre-invasion parachute jump in Normandy and combat jump in Holland during World War II, the 101st Airborne Division was reactivated at Fort Campbell on September 21, 1956. Early jump planes were the C-47 and C-46 (with two exits). Jumping from the right side of the C-46 was confusing initially and could result in a jumper's lanyard being wrapped around his neck.

Paratrooper, Fort Campbell, Kentucky

U. S. ARMY PHOTO

LANDING WAS:
PERFECT ☐
RUGGED ☐
SMOOTH ☐
.... ☐

MY .... JUMP
(No)

1C-H621

This linen postcard from Fort Campbell allowed a soldier to write to friends or family and describe his jump by checking blocks. He could also fill in the blank to show how many jumps he had made. The author has located a number of these cards but never one that has been filled in. It is safe to say not many landings in the old-type chutes were perfect.

"Bailing Out" over Fort Campbell, Ky.

Like the previous card, there is a place to check blocks on the back to describe your jump. Parts of Fort Campbell can be seen on the ground, including what appears to be a tactical landing strip directly below the center jumper. The army showed little interest in the airborne concept until Nazis succeeded with it. General Eisenhower presented the division with the Distinguished Unit Citation, the first time an entire unit had been so honored.

Recovering a Two and One-Half Ton Truck just Landed from Air Drop, at Fort Campbell, Kentucky

Soldiers are breaking away the special rigging used to facilitate the dropping of this two-and-a-half-ton truck at the 187th Drop Zone. The rigging is so constructed that it will distribute the shock of landing evenly throughout all members of the vehicle. These training exercises go on continuously at Fort Campbell.

In Vietnam during the late 1960s, one of the division's Bell UH-1 Hueys captures the essence of helicopter-mounted troops leaping to an already occupied hilltop. They gave up cover for high ground as the insertion was made onto a rocky parapet. The Huey came with single and twin engines. There were 5,000 UH-1s in Vietnam. By 1995, there were 1,000 army-wide, and in 2004, there were fewer than 150. The D/101st AHB flew this bird in Vietnam.

World War I ended before the airborne operation idea could be tested. The U.S. military did some experimentation in 1928 and 1929, and the Russians made jumps in 1936. Based on the recommendation of Maj. William Lee, the War Department formed the first U.S. Army parachute battalions, and in 1942, Gen. Leslie McNair formed two airborne divisions—the 101st and the 82nd.

Every aircraft and aviator imaginable has visited CAAF. Most of the astronauts stopped over as they went to and from Houston and Andrews Air Force Base; the largest aircraft in the U.S. Air Force inventory, the C-5, is a routine visitor, as is the space shuttle; a half-dozen presidents, Mickey Gilley, and this—the "vomit comet" used to train astronauts in weightlessness—are just a few of those having visited.

The Boeing Vertol CH-47 Chinook, the workhorse of army aviation, is a veteran of many thousands of hours of combat time. It was often the only mode of transportation during Desert Storm. In Bosnia, A Company, 5th Battalion, 159th Aviation Regiment's 16 aircraft flew 2,222 hours in six months. On November 2, 2003, near Fallujah, Iraq, 1st Lt. Brian Slavenas, CWO Bruce Smith, and 13 passengers were killed when their Chinook was attacked.

This early 1980s postcard shows a UH-1 Iroquois (Huey) with a jeep sling loaded. There are other cards showing the aircraft and its load in the air. A flight crewman lies on his stomach in the open door, checking the M-151 sling load. In 2004, veterans and new soldiers alike of the 1st Brigade learned to rig cargo nets during sling load training at Bastogne Baseball Field.

This modern postcard was produced by Clarksville's foto-1. Information on the back states that organized tours of the museum begin at Gate Four. The top left photograph is of a division run that is conducted regularly and led by the CG. At top right is the placement of a wreath honoring soldiers who have made the ultimate sacrifice, and the lower image is of an AH-1 Cobra gunship flying into the sunset.

Greetings from Fort Campbell, Kentucky

These are C-124 Globemasters positioned on keyholes at the south end of CAAF. Prior to the new breed of aircraft—the C-5, C-130, and C-141—these were the Air Force workhorses. The Globemaster could carry 90 combat-equipped troops, 70,000 pounds of cargo, or combinations of the two. With its removable upper deck, the aircraft was one of the most versatile of its time and ideal for moving soldiers.

Comical cards have enjoyed considerable popularity with the military (especially the army) since World War II. They poked fun at living in a tactical field environment and were often risqué. There have been many female soldiers go through Jump School, but only one has made a combat jump (and that one was questionable). There were a number of women in the Fort Campbell Parachute Club.

THINGS ARE SURE "LOOKING UP" FOR ME!

The Apache is what Lt. Col. Dick Cody (now a lieutenant general) fired the first shots of Desert Storm from. The anti-armor helicopter includes in its arsenal the Sidewinder and Sidearm (far left and far right); Mistral air-to-air missiles (foreground); 1,200 rounds of 30-mm ammunition; 76 2.75-inch/70-mm rockets; 16 Hellfire anti-tank missiles (on inboard pylon stations); and wingtip-mounted Stinger air-to-air missiles. David Petraeus followed Cody as Fort Campbell's CG.

AWESOME FIREPOWER

DESERT OPERATIONS

Sikorsky's UH-60L Black Hawks, like the ones flown by 4-3 Aviation, lift off in the terrain notorious for causing "brown-outs." The army's front-line utility helicopter, capable of moving 105-mm howitzers and 30 rounds of ammunition, was first flown in 1974. A service life extension program began in 1999. You can hang 16 Hellfire missiles on this bird and store an additional 16 internally.

All army aviation flight training is consolidated at Fort Rucker, Alabama (named for Col. Edmund Rucker, a Confederate officer and honorary general). Pilots trained here never forget the graduating class fly-by. Mother Rucker is located in the wiregrass country of lower Alabama, near the tiny town of Daleville.

An unknown person created this postcard. The sign says, "D Company 229 ATK HEL BN Guthrie Field" and has the 101st patch on it. The message on the back says, "There was CAAF, Sabre, and all the tactical sites for Fort Campbell's 600 rotary wing A/C. But, where is this?"

CAAF was built in 1942 as a U.S. Army Air Corps station. From World War II until 1959, it belonged to the U.S. Air Force. Much of CAAF's early history is lost. An aircrew man taxies a 6/101 Black Hawk to a parking spot at CAAF. Snowstorms can create whiteout conditions.

Serving in what is reputed to be one of the most stressful jobs in the world, both military and civilian air controllers are employed at CAAF. The old tower was vacated in the 1980s, when this new one was completed. In the event of a fire in these towers, air controllers' only means of egress would be from the catwalk down a fall-restraint cable.

The External Stores Support System (ESSS) extends the Black Hawk's range up to 1,150 nautical miles. In 1994, the 50th Air Ambulance flew UH-60 rescue missions hoisting East Tennessee residents stranded in snowstorms. In some cases, it was necessary to use a jungle penetrator to reach those stranded. On November 15, 2003, the collision of two Black Hawks over Mosul, Iraq, took the lives of 17 Screaming Eagle soldiers—at this writing that remains the division's deadliest day in Iraq.

Four Fort Campbell soldiers rappel at the same time in this photo postcard of the 1980s.

Fort Campbell is home to more than 600 helicopters. A few of those are seen here, tied down on an apron on the back of CAAF. Farmland and forests surround CAAF, making birds and deer a hazard to pilots during approach or departure.

Other branches of the military have jump teams, but all pale when compared to the army's Golden Knights. Their transport aircraft is shown here during one of many visits to Fort Campbell. In 1954, Sergeant Sounders of the 11th Airborne Division, Fort Campbell, was a Golden Knight. Parachute clubs at army posts served as a feeder system for the Golden Knights. Unfortunately, the once-popular Fort Campbell Parachute Club is closed.

A crewman can be seen walking through a C-5 parked at CAAF. Using front and rear cargo openings, loading and off-loading can take place at the same time.

In February 1992, Bill Harralson, the post's deputy Public Affairs Officer, reported a Chinook assigned to the 7th Battalion had dropped its load (an HMMWV) somewhere in Kentucky. It was located four days later, a total loss, and was returned to the post.

The AH-64D Apache is equipped with the Longbow Fire Control Radar, cutting-edge digital avionics, and more powerful engines than its predecessors. This bird is designed to operate in all sorts of adverse weather and in battlefield conditions. These are Apaches participating in a brigade exercise at National Training Center (NTC) in the 1990s. Brownouts are common in desert terrain. Several units including the 3/101 fly the Apache.

Jane!
these guys are being extracted by
helocopter....its one of those high
risk training exercises that we
monitor closely.

SPIES and FRIES are acronyms that deal with quickly inserting and extracting teams of soldiers from places where landing a helicopter is impractical or impossible. This photograph of Air Assault School students was provided to Jane Kelly, daughter of the Austin Peay State University basketball coach, to complement a college paper she was working on.

Two troops can be seen fast-roping into a training area from a Black Hawk. Notice others in the door ready to leave the aircraft. Fort Campbell units hone this technique and a number of others at the Air Assault School.

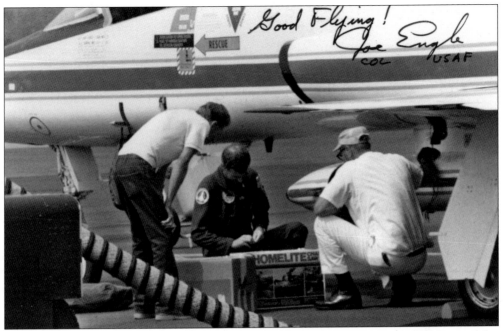

This is NASA's F-104 Starfighter, first acquired in 1956 on one of many visits to CAAF. In this image, from left to right, are Bob Marshall, CAAF; Joe Engle, veteran astronaut; and Transient Alert employee John Gafford. Dick Scobee, Judy Resnik, and many other astronauts often came into CAAF.

The original Flying Tigers (with shark teeth painted on planes) fought the Japanese over China and Burma in 1941. In 1944, Robert Prescott founded the Flying Tigers Airfreight Lines, which has always been closely associated with the army. Fort Campbell's 229th Aviation Regiment (Attack), which flies AH-64s, is also called the Flying Tigers. Here jacks and jennies (male and female donkeys) are being put aboard a Flying Tiger aircraft at CAAF bound for Afghanistan.

Unfortunately, aviation disasters are recurring in the military. While Fort Campbell has had more than her share of them, the numbers are miniscule when compared to the hours flown. Helicopters do not have the forgiving nature of small fixed-wing aircraft.

This image shows a portion of the aftermath of a mid-air collision of two helicopters at Fort Campbell. The list of Fort Campbell aviation fatalities is lengthy. Lt. Col. Michael J. McMahon, originally of Fort Campbell, was killed in a plane crash in Afghanistan in November 2004.

Maj. Gen. (later Lt. Gen.) Bennie Peay often flew in this U-21 Ute. The message on the card mentions the African American soldier who beat his wife to death with a baseball bat and left her unclothed body on Missouri Avenue (now Wickham Avenue). He was flown from CAAF on this aircraft. The "Welcome" sign and the Warthog that has just made a wheels-up landing in the background produce a little irony. The crash crew is foaming the bird down.

Taken in the late 1970s, this image shows a huge parking apron in the foreground. The cantonment area can be seen at the top of the photograph. It was—and is—rare to find this parking area void of aircraft.

This is part of the Assumption of Command ceremony for newly assigned CAAF commander Colonel Shepard on September 3, 1968. Shepard is on the right. Maj. Gen. Melvin Zais is beside him.

This is Lt. Gen. William C. Westmoreland (former Fort Campbell CG) when he was CG, XVIII Airborne Corps, Fort Bragg, North Carolina. The photograph is by Sgt. R. M. Wallace of Post Signal Photo Lab in Fort Bragg.

Three

TRAINING

The old Army jeeps, We killed over 1200 soldiers in these over the years. They rolled over easily because of the short wheel base

Two configurations of the M–151 (the famous army jeep) are shown here. When the army began to phase them out in the 1980s, they removed all hazardous wastes (including radioactive items) and cut the jeeps in half before auctioning them off to civilians. Civilians are clever—they purchased them, welded the two halves back together, and drove them.

Fort Campbell's engineering units are some of the army's most storied. The 41st Engineering Company and 20th Engineering Battalion worked at Milan Arsenal in the 1980s building a five-float-raft movable bridge. The new 326th Brigade Troops Battalion formed in 2004. Sgt. Hasan Akbar of the 326th was accused of the March 22, 2003, grenade incident at Camp Pennsylvania, Kuwait, in which two fellow soldiers were killed and 14 injured.

In World War II, famed war-poster artist Jes W. Schlaikjer rendered the historical painting used on this postcard. Military police units assigned to Fort Campbell have included the 716th MP Battalion, 1000th Criminal Investigation Command (CID) Battalion, 31st MP Detachment, 163rd MP Detachment, and the 101st MPs. In the December 2004 issue of *Reader's Digest*, Christine Bellavia tells the story of her husband, Joseph, one of the Fort Campbell MPs killed on October 16, 2003, in Karbala, Iraq.

The Schlaikjer 1943 original of this is in the collection of the National Infantry Museum. "Charlie" captured members of the 2nd Battalion, 501st Infantry Regiment in 1970, when their helicopter was ambushed and crashed. In 2002, the 2nd Battalion, 187th Infantry Regiment guarded air bases in Afghanistan. The soldiers of the 3rd Brigade Combat Team (Task Force Rakkasans) are entitled to the "Eagle Sandwich"—a combat patch on the right shoulder and a division patch on the left.

Special Forces is "the job" for tough adventure junkies. Fort Campbell's 160th Special Operations Aviation Regiment (Airborne) is reputed to have some of the army's best pilots. There are also approximately 2,500 soldiers from 5th Special Forces Group (Airborne) at Fort Campbell. M.Sgt. Jefferson Davis was a member of 5th Special Forces when he and 11 other Fort Campbell soldiers were killed in an aircraft crash in the Philippines on May 24, 2002.

U.S. ARMY RANGERS

Rangers led the way at Omaha Beach and again during Operation Overlord at Utah Beach. Much of the Ranger training today uses a new breed of military simulator, part video game and part Hollywood sound stage, called Joint Fires and Effects Trainer System, or JFETS. In 2005, the army (including the Rangers) is going to an all-in-one camouflage uniform. The army makeover will cost $3.4 billion and be phased in at Fort Campbell over the next three years.

SERVICE ABOVE SELF

MEDICAL DEPARTMENT
UNITED STATES ARMY

The era of modern military medical treatment on the battlefield became a reality in World War II. In Vietnam, medics were often singled out for heroism in treating casualties. Maj. Patrick Brady was one of 245 Vietnam-era Medal of Honor winners. He was the commander of 326th Medical Battalion at Fort Campbell, an aviator, and eventually a major general.

The U.S. Army Reserve Command (USARC) and Fort Campbell have a great relationship. During times of crisis, reserve units are made ready and deployed from Fort Campbell. The 81st Reserve Support Command of Birmingham, Alabama, falls in the geographical area supported by Fort Campbell.

At the end of Eighteenth Street just across Range Road, soldiers could be found in combat gear negotiating the infiltration course. This rite of passage includes low crawling and back crawling and is one of the final challenges in the Basic Combat Training courses.

A practice explosive devise goes off in the immediate area of soldiers on the infiltration course. Trainees made a 75-yard crawl that gave them a taste of moving around emplaced demolitions and under live machine-gun fire overhead. Fort Campbell has always provided some of the most realistic training available.

Advanced Training at Fort Campbell, Ky.

Soldiers involved in advanced basic training receive instruction and experience with the lightweight, recoilless bazooka issued to soldiers at the squad and platoon levels. The original idea for this weapon is attributed to Dr. Robert Goddard, of rocket research fame. This weapon made a single soldier as powerful as a tank. One of the highest compliments is imitation, and the bazooka led to the 12-inch Lefty McGill action figure.

KENTUCKY NATIONAL GUARD

Kentucky National Guard and Reserve units often train at Fort Campbell. This is part of the 1st Battalion, 123rd Armor, originally constituted as the 1st Kentucky Volunteer Cavalry and the 2nd Kentucky Volunteer Infantry on May 22, 1846. Units include HHC 1st Battalion, 123rd Army Reserve (AR), 35th Infantry Division (ID) Paducah; Detachment 1 HHC 1st Battalion, 123rd AR, 35th ID Hickman; and Companies A, B, C, and D 1st Battalion, 123rd AR, 35th ID of Marion, Hopkinsville, Madisonville, and Benton, respectfully.

GREETINGS FROM FORT CAMPBELL
ON THE TENNESSEE-KENTUCKY STATE LINE

Greetings from Fort Campbell—the top portion of the card shows a mass parachute jump, while the lower portion shows a tank-configured flamethrower. The message on the back discusses an accident in which two people deliberately hit two young soldiers who were riding a motorcycle. It goes on to say one soldier lost a leg and the occupants of the car have been charged with attempted murder.

Rifle Bayonet Practice, Fort Campbell, Ky.

The narrative on the back of this 1968 Fort Campbell card states, "This huge installation, constructed in WW II, has been expanded and is now one of the main training bases in the nation. The Third Army Training Center graduates thousands of ground force trainees yearly. Soldiers receive training in the use of close combat weapons."

Realistic Training, Fort Campbell, Kentucky

A napalm air strike neutralizes an "enemy position" for a "mop-up" by ground troops at Fort Campbell. Napalm became a politically charged word when it was widely used in World War II, Korea, and Vietnam. It is a fiery concoction made of jellied accelerant (soap powder and gasoline) causing the syrupy substance to stick to its target and burn slowly. Inventor Dr. Louis Fieser of Harvard and manufacturer Dow Chemical Company both took a lot of heat for their roles in making napalm available.

50

Rifle Squad Training, Fort Campbell, Ky.

Soldiers are doing rifle squad training under a smoke screen. Usually a 12-man rifle squad was made up of a squad leader, two scouts, an automatic rifle team of three men, five riflemen, and an assistant squad leader who is usually the antitank grenadier.

"The Battle of Fort Campbell, Ky."

This piece of equipment is an eight-inch self-propelled howitzer. In their time, these were "big guns." Howitzer is from the Czech word *houfnice*. The M-110 traverses 60 degrees and was the most accurate artillery weapon system in the U.S. Army arsenal. Today much of the howitzer firing is done indoors on simulators.

The M-48 tanks shown here are on a hot firing line at Fort Campbell. Different tanks have main weapons positioned differently. On the M-48, .50-caliber machine guns are mounted atop the cupola. This tank was developed from the M-47 General Patton tank and was a mainstay in Vietnam. The A2C model had a gasoline engine and was prone to fire. As a result of lessons learned, the A3 model was given a diesel engine.

This fortified outpost position is occupied by an anti-tank platoon. Defense weapons include a 90-mm recoilless rifle in the front right, a M-16 rifle front left, and a "gun jeep" equipped with a 106-mm recoilless rifle in the background.

Marksmanship Practice on Rifle Range

The "Always First" 1st Brigade trained on these ranges. Formed in 1963 at Fort Campbell, the 1st Brigade departed for Vietnam in 1965. Unlike other units in Vietnam, they did not establish a base camp for some time and earned the nickname "Nomads of Vietnam." The 1st Brigade's Long Range Reconnaissance Patrol (LRRP) carried M-16s and participated in Operation Eagle Bait near Phan Rang in July 1966. They wore the tiger stripe uniforms.

The 105-mm howitzer was the most used field artillery piece in World War II. The 3rd Brigade's Red Knights are being instructed in communications and firing techniques as they send hot steel down range. In the mid-1980s, the M-102 howitzer replaced the 105. This system was often placed in a gun pit. Environmentalists are concerned with concentrations of explosives residue in and around craters caused by the 105.

Six Gun Salute, Fort Campbell, Ky.

In this photograph, a firing battery of six 105-mm howitzers is drawn in a salute formation. It is no small wonder artillerymen often have premature hearing losses. A mortar round in Vietnam killed 1st Lt. Bob Kalsu, an artillery officer of the 101st, in 1970. Before he was an artillery officer, he was an offensive guard for the Buffalo Bills. Bob Jr. was born two days after he was killed.

Joint Readiness Training Center (JRTC), moved from Fort Chaffee, Arkansas, to Fort Polk, Louisiana, in 1991. This card shows some of the tactical training Fort Campbell soldiers get while at JRTC. At Chaffee, there were M-551 Sheridan tanks outfitted to replicate Soviet T-72 tanks.

Soldiers pause before assaulting the remainder of a building during intensive Urban Warfare exercises. Clearing and securing urban areas (often fierce house-to-house fighting) has become a major emphasis on Fort Campbell ranges due to worldwide mission requirements. It was a procedure 101st soldiers used in Panama, Grenada, and currently in Iraq. Similar to the "tire cities" at Fort Campbell and in Saudi Arabia, this training is dangerous.

Fort Campbell's 101st Division Artillery (Divarty) used the M-109 155-mm self-propelled howitzer. It is the standard direct-support artillery weapon for Fort Campbell's armored and mechanized infantry units. Steve Crawford took this photograph.

The NBC Reconnaissance System Vehicle (Fox) is highly mobile, armored, and equipped with integrated NBC (nuclear, biological, and chemical) detection, warning, and communications systems. Many division chemical personnel trained in this vehicle, originally developed by the Germans. Our version was modeled after the FUCHS. The M-93A has a crew of three and the M-93 a crew of four. The Fox first entered the army in 1998 and is very expensive to operate and to maintain.

The Heavy Equipment Mobility Tactical Truck (HEMTT) is the backbone of the army's battlefield cargo support. There are some five different configurations in use, and most of those are in the Fort Campbell inventory. Perhaps best known is the tanker M-978 that replaced many two-and-a-half and five-ton trucks in 1982. Manufactured by Oshkosh Truck in Oshkosh, Wisconsin, it is capable of 57 miles per hour maximum speed, with a 300-mile cruising range.

This HMMWV (touted as the Super Jeep) was fielded at Fort Campbell in 1987. PFC Thomas Cruse (not to be confused with actor Tom Cruise) was first to drive it. In 2004, the army was rushing to provide soldiers in Iraq the "up-armored" HMMWVs to minimize casualties from so-called improvised explosive devices (IEDs). IEDs commonly consist of a 152-mm artillery shell in concrete that is placed along the road and detonated by remote control. That is how Fort Campbell's 1st Lt. Joshua Hurley was killed in Mosul, Iraq.

This is an Armored Vehicle Launched Bridge (AVLB). This and other types of mobile bridging equipment are used by Fort Campbell engineers to provide units with immediate crossing capabilities when they encounter water or hostile terrain. The AVLB is a turret-less M-60A1. Anniston Army Depot (ANAD) was the contractor for the system. It has a replacement cost of more than $700,000.

Squad mates are shown firing a shoulder-launched Multipurpose Assault Weapon (Stinger) at a target during a training exercise. This weapon is a portable anti-armor rocket launcher. Earlier tank killers used by Fort Campbell soldiers included the Mauser M-1918 AT rifle and rifle grenades with shaped, charged warheads.

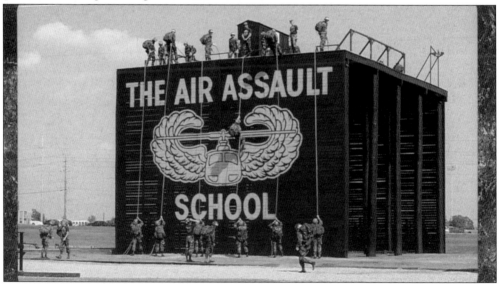

Maj. Gen. Sidney Berry, CG of the 101st Airborne Division (Airmobile), approved a new badge and school in January 1974 so that soldiers might earn the forerunner of today's silver wings. In October 1974, the division became the 101st Airborne Division (Air Assault) and the badge became the Air Assault Badge. Renamed in 1994 for distinguished Vietnam veteran CSM Walter Sabalauski, the Air Assault School has a 70-percent completion rate.

During a 1990s NTC rotation, the 101st had 50-plus soldiers go down with heat injuries while training in Mock IV gear similar to what is seen on the postcard. Daytime temperatures were in the 130-degree range. During all Middle Eastern deployments, intelligence warned that Iraq might resort to chemical warfare, so 101st troops were issued, and often wore, full chemical protective gear. Iraq did not have or use chemical weapons.

We couldnt Change the wheel base & stop the rollovers...So we put rollover bars on it & installed seatbelts... no fatalities since.

The M-151 was the backbone of the army and synonymous with soldiers. They were capable of speeds of 65 miles per hour but had a narrow wheelbase and were easily turned over. More than 1,200 soldiers were killed in accidents involving the jeep (mostly rollovers). Once they were equipped with rollover bar, seatbelts, and netting, there were no recorded fatalities resulting from rollovers.

Named by Brig. Gen. Holger N. Toftoy, former Redstone Arsenal commander, this weapon was capable of delivering a nuclear warhead. Developed in the 1950s, the Honest John was the army's first nuclear surface-to-surface rocket and brought about pentomic structure (a reorganizaation of units from 1957 to 1959 as a result of the development of nuclear weapons). Replaced by the Lance and Little John missiles in the 1970s, it became obsolete in the early 1980s. Fort Campbell's 377th Artillery Battalion had the Little John rocket, which accommodated nuclear or conventional warheads.

The tube-launched, optically tracked, wire-guided (TOW) missile is hurdled from its launcher mounted atop the HMMWV. This is a force-protection weapon essential for deploying units, particularly combat service support (CSS) units, who are among the first to deploy and last to be redeployed.

This is the M-9 Armored Combat Earthmover (ACE) crossing a temporary bridge emplacement during a training exercise. On the battlefield, it would speed ahead of other combat units to neutralize enemy obstacles. The ACE is transportable in C-130 and larger aircraft.

The Palletized Load System (PLS) has an integral load-handling system that provides self-loading and unloading capability. A very capable off-road vehicle, it can deliver a 16-and-a-half-ton payload almost anywhere. Not available to the army until 1993, it provides long-haul, rapid movement of all classes of supplies in tactical environments.

The armored personnel carriers (APCs) seen on the CAAF flight line are M-113A1s. The C-141 that they were aboard is seen in the background.

An Arrow Air aircraft went down in Gander, Newfoundland, on December 12, 1985. Also lost were 258 Fort Campbell soldiers. Arrow Air was founded in 1950 and was often a contract carrier for troops out of CAAF. These are soldiers deploying around that time.

These are antipersonnel mines that spray shrapnel into a "guaranteed casualty area." The M–18A1 is dangerous to 250 meters. It contains 700 steel spheres with a one-and-a-half-pound layer of composition C–4 explosive. It projects a fan-shaped pattern. According to Human Rights Watch, worldwide—in places like Kuwait, Afghanistan, and Iraq—30 to 40 percent of the tens of thousands killed annually by these types of mines are women and children. Fort Campbell's Claymore Field is where post rugby teams play.

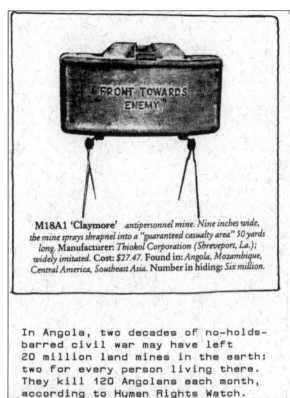

M18A1 'Claymore' *antipersonnel mine. Nine inches wide, the mine sprays shrapnel into a "guaranteed casualty area" 50 yards long.* **Manufacturer:** *Thiokol Corporation (Shreveport, La.); widely imitated.* **Cost:** *$27.47.* **Found in:** *Angola, Mozambique, Central America, Southeast Asia.* **Number in hiding:** *Six million.*

In Angola, two decades of no-holds-barred civil war may have left 20 million land mines in the earth: two for every person living there. They kill 120 Angolans each month, according to Human Rights Watch.

Tank turrets often rotated on to drivers standing in their open hatches. The M-1 provided the increased capacity required by more lethal and agile opposing tank forces. It is the army's principal combat tank, with a mission to close and destroy. Equipped with a mine plow, it entered the army in 1980 but was untested in combat until the 1991 Gulf War. The M-1 has replaced most of the tanks once assigned to Fort Campbell.

All soldiering is dangerous, but few missions are more high risk that fuel handling. When this tanker burned during night operations near Gate 10, it sent a skyward plume that could be seen in Clarksville. In October 2004, the 343rd Quartermaster Company (a reserve unit) refused an order to move fuel through a dangerous area in Iraq—some of that fuel was needed by 101st soldiers.

Col. J. Tom Denney, garrison commander, and Marvin Emmons, safety manager, change the Safety Office Traffic Fatality Board to indicate the post has gone 101 days without a traffic fatality. That did not happen often, and soldiers were awarded a day off when it did. The year the division returned from Vietnam, Fort Campbell soldiers were involved in more than 70 traffic fatalities. Marvin has passed away; Denney and his lovely wife, Sandra, still reside in Clarksville. The author stands on the far side of the sign.

Bayonet and pugilist competition is antiquated, as today's infantrymen are equipped with integrated fighting systems such as the Land Warrior Systems (LWS) and Objective Crew Served Weapons (OCSW). Meanwhile, more high-tech equipment is being developed at the Army Research Center in Natick, Massachusetts.

In a field near CAAF, soldiers take shelter behind their vehicles as a Chinook lifts off with the artillery piece and HMWWV they have just finished sling loading. Aircrews have a more affectionate name for the Chinook but it would not be prudent to print it.

In September 1989, equipment was moved by rail to Lock C on the Cumberland River, where 42 barges departed for Fort Smith, Arkansas. It was the largest inland water move since World War II. Bill Ferguson was the installation transportation officer (ITO) overseeing the operation. On the return trip, the 101st sent a number of pieces of rolling stock to the bottom of the Mississippi River.

A Fort Campbell soldier treks across the "dust bowl" at NTC looking for his new quarters. Orthopedic surgeons and chiropractors who treat soldiers with bad backs at Blanchfield Hospital likely look at this and shake their heads.

Fatigue (common during an field training exercise, or FTX) caused this accident that killed two Fort Campbell soldiers and critically injured a third. Aerial photographs taken by investigators showed the driver veered off the road on his right, overcorrected, and flipped the vehicle several times on the other side of the road.

These soldiers are firing the Dragon. Ammo, rockets, and so on that misfired or were not used had to be returned to Range Control. That did not always happen. According to PAO Maj. Randy Schoel, Sgt. Morgan Lee Spiers of 227th General Support Company was taken into custody in April 1989 for removing thousands of rounds of ammo and related equipment from on-post.

Global thunder is heard for miles around in two states when the U.S. Air Force supports army exercises at Fort Campbell. Here an aircraft drops 500-pound bombs on a training area.

In 1981, Bob Goodwin, director at Training and Audiovisual Support Center (TASC), did six different prints of Fort Campbell soldiers. Beverly Maki updated the prints by putting in Kevlar helmets and other modern gear. Soldiers were occasionally presented with one of these prints when they were transferred. Helen (known by close friends as Sam) Zachry was another talented TASC artist.

Four

PALADINA AND PRATT MUSEUM POSTCARDS

Like thunderbolts from the sky, members of the 101st conduct an air assault raid deep in the heart of Fort Campbell. This is done as a public demonstration during Week of the Eagle and routinely as unit training. Troops can be seen scampering from UH-60s.

This postcard from retired 1st Sgt. Gene Paladina to the author was the result of an advertisement the author ran in *Army Times* in 1984. Gene writes from the Eagle's Nest (his home on Airport Road near the post) where he is a self-appointed historian for Fort Campbell. Gene has a serious hearing loss now, and his sister lives with him. He logged many parachute jumps while assigned to Fort Campbell.

Across from CBR (a training area), soldiers of the 101st are rappelling from a UH-60 Black Hawk helicopter during squad training, in which soldiers respond to individual tap outs. The Swiss seat configuration is one of the most popular for army rappellers. Soldiers from other units are often seen double-timing on nearby roads.

This is the C-119 Flying Boxcar displayed in front of Pratt Museum. It is the grandchild of the C-82. While you exited below the prop wash in the C-119, a weak exit would still result in the paratrooper impacting the side of the aircraft. An AH-56 Cheyenne helicopter is to the right and behind the C-119.

Paratroopers must believe what Alan Seeger said: "I have a rendezvous with death at some disputed barricade, and I to my pledged word am true, I shall not fail that rendezvous." This is the old T-10 chute, which was the first of the parabolic chutes and had the anti-inversion net added. They sometimes opened untangled, sometimes not, but when they did open there was a severe opening shock. The rucksack tab lowering the rucksack can be seen.

This early 1960s view (dated by the old-type helmet and name tag in white) shows a 101st soldier armed with an M-16 staring into the skies as fellow Fort Campbell soldiers descend in T–7s. They have jumped from C-123s in V formation. Aircraft would fly nap of the earth (NOE) until jumpers got their five-minute warning, when all aircraft would "head for the top." All jumps were by static line. If the aircraft echelon was not correct, it could result in jumping into the path of another aircraft.

Fort Campbell Military Police stand guard in the sands of Saudi Arabia during Operation Desert Shield of the Persian Gulf War.

On June 5, 1990, during the Week of the Eagle festivities, the 101st conducted this air assault demonstration. A soldier under camouflage net can be seen at the left, while a simulator explodes on the right. Air assault would involve every type of helicopter stationed at Fort Campbell. Maj. Gen. John Cushman began Week of the Eagle in 1973 as a way to recruit soldiers.

Soldiers exit in tandem from a Black Hawk. In the early 1990s, the author investigated a fatality resulting from a 90-foot fall from a Black Hawk. Other young soldiers have died in rappelling accidents at Queen's Bluff on the Cumberland River and at local rock quarries, both popular sites for rappelling. Belay men can be seen on the ground maintaining a tight rappel rope.

Air assault helicopters of all types dot the flight line of King Fahd International Airport, Saudi Arabia, during the early months of Operation Desert Shield. This field will remind many of one in Danang that looked much the same.

Artillery pieces belonging to the 320th Field Artillery are sling loaded under Black Hawks for an exercise at Yamoto DZ (drop zone). The M-105 has been replaced with the 107.

This is Task Force 3 of the 502nd at the dedication ceremony for the 248 soldiers who died in Gander, Newfoundland, as they returned from MFO (Multinational Force and Observers) duty in the Sinai. The plane crash occurred on take off. Maj. Gen. Burton Patrick oversaw this dedication for next of kin. Color-bearing units are also seen here. President and Nancy Reagan came to Fort Campbell to show their respects and view the 248 Canadian Maples planted along Twenty-Sixth Street.

Old Glory has flown half-mast at 101st Headquarters far too many times. It was lowered for former CGs of Fort Campbell; chairs of the Joint Chief of Staffs; the 248 soldiers killed in Gander; and always on Memorial and Veterans Day for the nation's fallen heroes. It is still lowered on the anniversary of Kennedy's death and goes back up at noon. This is the large garrison flag. During bad weather, a smaller "weather flag" replaces it.

This memorial monument is dedicated to the soldiers of the 327th Infantry Regiment who have given their lives for their country. CSM Jackie D. Armstrong was in attendance for the dedication. Readers may recall when the story broke of atrocities by the 327th in Vietnam's Duc Pho Valley in 1967. In August 2003, SPC Farao Letufuga of the 327th was killed when he fell from a building in Mosul, Iraq.

Hopkinsville also honored Task Force 3, 502nd Infantry Battalion soldiers who died in the Gander crash. The idea for a memorial all started with Janice Johnston, a 13-year-old Canadian girl. The Gander mayor and Amy Nichols Redmon, wife of one of the victims of the plane crash, attended the dedication.

Gen. Maxwell Taylor's aircraft for the Normandy Invasion led the 101st Airborne Division across the English Channel on the night of June 6, 1944. This "Brass Hat" is a replica of that C-47 and has a similar paint job. It is displayed in the outdoor exhibit park of the Pratt Museum. The Pratt Museum will be replaced by the 80,000-square-foot Wings of Liberty Military Museum planned for a 24-acre campus along Highway 41A.

This memorial honors the Screaming Eagles for the liberation of the city of Veghel during the World War II invasion of Holland. On September 17, 1961, the Dutch government brought 10,000 tulips to CG C. W. G. Rich and created the Dutch Living Garden of Memory honoring the 101st casualties who participated in Operation Market Garden. Located where the MP building is at Gate 4, it fell into neglect when the Division went to Vietnam. A few flowers were saved and are in the museum's outdoor exhibit.

This monument honors the 187th Rakkasans, who evolved from the old 173rd (sky soldiers). The division's 3rd Battalion, 187th Infantry Regiment is the only airborne or air assault infantry battalion to have fought in the four major wars of the past 50 years. They have had hundreds of soldiers die in combat.

Camp Eagle I was base camp of the 101st in Vietnam. Camp Eagle II was base camp during the Persian Gulf War and a marshalling area for Company B, 8th Battalion, 101st Aviation Regiment. In 1990, the 101st went to defend Saudi Arabia, and Camp Eagle II was created out of necessity as a place where Fort Campbell soldiers could properly acclimate to the desert. Col. Ted Purdom, commander 2nd Brigade, escorted Bob Hope around Camp Eagle II's Bedouin tent city.

This memorial monument is in honor of those who served with the 11th Airborne Division from February 25, 1943, to July 1, 1958. The card is postmarked Fort Campbell and was mailed by Gene Paladina. This monument is located in the outdoor Exhibit Park at Pratt Museum. The 11th was also known as the "Flying Red Assholes," and battalion muster often went like this: "10 old AWOLs and 5 new AWOLs, Sir!"

This monument is dedicated to the "Strike" 2, 502nd Infantry Battalion soldiers killed in action in Vietnam from 1967 to 1972. In attendance on the day of the commissioning of this monument were General Silvasey; Ben Lam, a Vietnamese civilian Kit Carson scout who spoke perfect English; Col. Tom Taylor, 101st veteran Maxwell Taylor's son; and the legendary Col. Frank Dietrich, who was awarded three Combat Infantry Badges and after whom the fictional character Sergeant Berkley in Ross Carter's book *Those Devils in Baggy Pants* was patterned.

This is the Screaming Eagle Memorial Monument at Arlington National Cemetery. Paladina took the photograph on Memorial Day of 1989. Dedicated in August 1977, this national monument is within view of the Lincoln Memorial.

Located between the R. F. Sink Library and the head shed, this stone celebrates the 25th anniversary of Fort Campbell's Vietnam-era soldiers. The library was named for Col. "Bourbon Bob" Sink, who led the 506th Parachute Infantry Regiment (PIR). He would retire a lieutenant general. Clarksville city councilperson Mary Nell Wooten was librarian here for a number of years.

Five

STRUCTURES

Division Headquarters Building
CAMP CAMPBELL, KENTUCKY
Photograph by Signal Corps, U.S. Army

This is an early-1940s free-franked postcard from a Signal Corps photograph of the HQ Building. These cards were printed courtesy of Southern Bell Telephone and Telegraph Company Incorporated. Cpl. Everett Peterman, Troop C, 33rd CW, sent this to folks back home in Bluefield, West Virginia.

This is Building 100. It served as the HQ for 12th Armored Division (Hellcats) and remains the HQ Building today. In September 1942, the Hellcats activated at Camp Campbell under the command of Maj. Gen. Carlos Brewer. Germans dubbed the 12th the "Suicide Division." They were secretly transferred from the Seventh Army to Patton's Third and renamed "Mystery Division." They were credited with taking 72,243 prisoners while suffering 5,976 casualties. Decommissioned in 1945, they never returned to Fort Campbell.

Fort Campbell and 101st HQ Building has changed very little since it was built in the early 1940s. The U-shaped building directly behind it is the Clifford C. Sims Guest House. The CG's UH-1 Huey is sitting on the front lawn. The CG, his staff, and the occasional guest would walk to the aircraft for flights to other places on post.

82

In the 1960s, clubs on the post included Club Indiana, Club Bastogne, the Top 5 Club, Club Jinmachi, Club 32, Essayon Club, Service Club No. 2 and the O Club. Officers' support for their club began to wane in the 1980s and 1990s, and Gen. Bennie Peay cautioned young officers that if membership continued to fall off, the Officers Club would go away. It did.

Officers' Club, Camp Campbell, Ky.-Tenn.

This is Officer's Club number 1 at Camp Campbell, Kentucky–Tennessee. The message on the card says, "They just built a big section onto this club. It's almost twice as big now."

The message on the back says the following about Service Club No. 2: "This is a typical service club—where we eat. Right lower is library and left is the cafeteria. The recreation room is in the center. There are around 10 of these kinds of buildings on a large camp. Sometimes more." At times there have been more than 10 Fort Campbell clubs operating at the same time.

This is an interior view of the club in the card above. This is the recreation room mentioned in the message.

The earliest postmark found on this set of cards was 1942. This is Chapel No. 1, Camp Campbell. Compare this to the next image. An Alaskan totem pole with a thunderbird atop it and three bands representing Normandy, Dutch, and Bastogne battles once stood in the chapel yard. Originally on Jumpy Johnson Field (where Losada Gym is now), it was moved twice (a portion cut off each time) and was last seen at Central Chapel.

This chapel is at Camp Ellis, Illinois. It appears the engineers used the same building plans for the chapel at Camp Campbell (above). The author located cards from many installations that appeared nearly identical.

Enlisted Men's Barracks and Mess Halls, Camp Campbell, Ky.–Tenn.

Enlisted men's barracks and mess halls are shown here. This very same card can be found identifying it as "Camp Breckinridge, Morganfield, Kentucky." In 2005, some of these buildings were (as had happened years before) sold for $100, $200, or $300. The buyer was responsible for moving it off post. Older buildings that migrated off post through this process can still be seen in the area.

In May 1966, Army General Order Number 161 directed the activation of a basic combat training center at Fort Campbell. A total of 500 World War II–vintage buildings were renovated to serve as trainee barracks. Two months later, the first 220 newly inducted soldiers arrived. At one time, there were 129 trailers for enlisted men located near Indiana and Fifty-Sixth Streets.

PHOTO BY U. S. ARMY SIGNAL CORPS   3B-H867

This open concept for barracks remained in use until the 1970s. Footlockers are at the ends of the beds. Boots can be seen under the beds, and uniforms hang neatly between the beds. There is a bookcase with books at the far end of the barracks between the doors. Vents for radiant heat can be seen down the center of the barracks. The photograph is by U.S. Signal Corps and is in stark contrast to soldiers' living quarters today.

Camp Campbell Post Office and Guest House, Camp Campbell, Ky.–Tenn.

The building in the foreground is the post office, and the one behind it is the guesthouse. The cars appear to be 1930s and 1940s models. On September 23, 1942, Camp Campbell, Tennessee, was re-designated Camp Campbell, Kentucky, thanks to Vice President Barkley (of Kentucky) in spite of the fact the majority of the post's 100,000 acres is in Tennessee.

Post Theatre, Fort Campbell, Kentucky

1C-H618

There have been many theatres on the post. Identified on the card as the Post Theatre, this is believed to be Mann Theatre, which still serves as a theatre. It is permanent, air-conditioned, and located at Kansas and Twenty-Sixth Streets. Wilson Theatre is also in operation and looks very similar.

War Department Theatre, Camp Campbell, Ky.–Tenn.

2B-H1268

This is the War Department Theatre No. 5, an extremely popular gathering place for Camp Campbell soldiers. All soldiers today own their own cars, and public transportation is available on post. Neither was the case in the 1940s and 1950s.

View of Motor Pool, Camp Campbell, Ky.-Tenn.

3B-H241

Some of these old motor pools have survived, while the concrete maintenance ramps were removed for environmental reasons in the early 1990s. The motor pool on the left has 17 small maintenance bays for jeeps while the ones on the right are configured with four larger bays.

General View of Hospital, Camp Campbell, Ky. Tenn.

3B-H240

Comprised of 53 buildings with seven-and-a-half miles of corridors on 72 acres, this is a general view of the "old" hospital. This card was free-franked in October 1943, when Pvt. Mac Goldfarb of the 59th Chemical Company mailed it to the La Martiniques of New York City. This is now the Military Police and Staff Judge Advocate Building.

U. S. Army Hospital, Fort Campbell, Ky.

The U.S. Army Hospital at Fort Campbell was one of the largest and best built for its time. It had over seven-and-a-half miles of hallways connecting some 53 buildings. Dr. Jane Grimes works at Blanchfield Army Community Hospital (BACH). Her mother worked at the U.S. Army Hospital. Many families have lengthy ties to Fort Campbell.

Post Chapel, Fort Campbell, Kentucky

Central Chapel, the new post chapel, would ensure "the spiritual needs of the military personnel are carefully supervised by highly trained, thoughtful and sincere officers of the Chaplain Corps." At one point, there were 10 chapels on post, including one at the stockade and one on CAAF.

Post Chapel, Fort Campbell, Kentucky

This appears to be another "new" post chapel.

Fort Campbell Post Exchange

The sign above the Fort Campbell Post Exchange contains the patches for the 101st and Third Army. The card states that "about 15 branch stores in the troop areas offer similar service on a smaller scale." Today this is the AAFES PXtra (Army and Air Forces Exchange Service PX Extra) in what amounts to a strip mall. In 2004, Fort Campbell planned the largest PX in the world. That plan is indicative of how the post is growing.

Ft. Campbell, Kentucky

The Pratt Museum honors and remembers all units that have served and trained at Fort Campbell. Among those represented are major units such as the 12th, 14th, and 20th Armored Divisions; the 11th Airborne Division; the 173rd Airborne Brigade (separate); and the 187th Airborne Regimental Combat Team. Active Fort Campbell units are also represented. Originally this was the 101st Airborne Division Museum.

The Directorate of Engineering and Housing (DEH) modified the old Air Assault Tower a number of times. Here they are replacing the top of the structure.

Six

SURROUNDING COMMUNITIES

BARRAGE BALLOON TRAINING CENTER — CAMP TYSON — PARIS, TENN.

World War II–era soldiers from Camp Campbell may recall Camp Tyson, near Paris, Tennessee. It was home for barrage balloon training. The balloons were tethered to earth around cities, military bases, and other locations to prevent attack by aircraft. Post-Intelligencer Print printed these cards. While it was not as popular as some of the other communities, some soldiers visited Paris, met and married local girls, and stayed when their enlistments were up.

Court House, Clarksville, Tenn.

Many a soldier has visited this old courthouse in Clarksville. They came to get license plates, pay taxes, and settle traffic tickets, and some to deal with more serious offences. Some, like the soldiers who murdered four Taco Bell employees in Clarksville in January 1994, came and were never allowed to go back to Fort Campbell or home.

APSU   Ft. Campbell

HEADQUARTERS
101 AIRBORNE DIVISION
(AIR ASSAULT) AND
FORT CAMPBELL

Clarksville, Tennessee

The author took these pictures in the early 1980s, and Beverly Maki created the postcard. Unnumbered soldiers and ex-soldiers have attended Austin Peay State University. Two such persons were father-and-son duo Ken Goble Sr. and Jr., who played football on the same APSU team. APSU now has a satellite branch on post. On the right, a Golden Knight delivers the colors to the CG at Post HQ.

The Royal York Hotel in downtown Clarksville is where Gen. Omar Bradley was a frequent visitor. Bradley was one of only six who held the title General of the Army—or less formally, a five-star. For the record, there is a higher rank, General of the Armies, held by only two men, Washington and Pershing. This is also where young ladies would lean out the windows of the hotel on military paydays and wave their undergarments at soldiers driving around the block.

Royal York Hotel-Clarksville, Tenn. E-8

Nearby Kentucky Lake provides soldiers the opportunity to boat, ski, fish, swim, and sunbathe. Unfortunately, many soldiers have drowned while participating in the same recreational events. The 160th frequently flies this area, and boats can be rented on post for use here.

The 49th Tennessee Infantry served and sadly surrendered here, as did other Confederate units. Once Fort Donelson fell, it was easy for the Union to advance to Clarksville, Nashville, and deeper into the South. The famed Blue Raider, Nathan Bedford Forrest, refused to surrender and went on to fight brilliantly throughout the war. Today Forrest's tactics are taught at West Point. Military history–minded soldiers often visit Fort Donelson. The Red River Raiders skirmish unit from Clarksville is shown on the card.

Dover has been home to many soldiers. The Cumberland River, Fort Donelson, and rural living appealed to soldiers who came from similar hometowns. Dover no longer looks like this, but it has not changed as much as most places. Many Fort Campbell retirees reside here.

The rural communities of Tiny Town and Guthrie appealed to some soldiers. The state-line community of Squig has always been popular with African American soldiers.

Hopkinsville and Clarksville have always vied for and shared those soldiers who chose to live off post. Clarksville is larger and is thought to offer more, but "Hoptown" is fast closing that gap. Joe and Patsy Woosley both retired from civil service at Fort Campbell and are Hoptown natives.

This is a Christian County, Kentucky, memorial to the 248 Fort Campbell soldiers who died on December 12, 1985. Les Filotas wrote *Improbable Cause* about the disaster. Theories include ice on the wings; 20 Special Forces soldiers aboard were trained in counter-terrorist missions and may have been targeted by terrorist missiles and Iran; and an explosion behind the last row of seats, perhaps from a souvenir. FBI files on the incident are still closed.

This Hopkinsville War Memorial Building on South Virginia Street was constructed in 1943 as a memorial to local citizens who made the supreme sacrifice for their country. It also functioned as a USO to serve the military personnel at nearby Camp Campbell. Since 1948, it has been a community center, and for many years it was Teen Town on Friday and Saturday nights.

Soldiers stayed at Hopkinsville's Ivory Tower Inn while on temporary duty assignments here from other installations, while awaiting housing at Fort Campbell, and with girlfriends. It had 75 rooms, a 150-seat restaurant, a lounge, and a pool. The popular motel was torn down several years ago, and the Heritage Bank now occupies this space.

Few soldiers who were ever stationed at Camp or Fort Campbell avoided the temptation to go to the big city—Nashville. There were more clubs, more restaurants, and more girls. There were also soldiers who did not go for the aforementioned reasons. Many went to see the Grand Ole Opry. The post has always had a good relationship with country music. Part of the Patsy Cline film *Sweet Dreams* was filmed at Fort Campbell.

T. Bird

BEEP! BEEP!

KBT-7580

MISS T BIRD &
LITTLE T-BIRDS
P. O. BOX 393
OAK GROVE, KY. 42262

Oak Grove is the community just outside the main gate. It is a Kentucky town but is poorly defined around the Kentucky-Tennessee state line. Many soldiers have been amateur radio operators and used QSL cards to notify other radio operators that their transmission had been received. Raymond J. (Jack) Elliott was Oak Grove's first mayor. Oak Grove's Cat West, an after-hours club, has been the focus of many controversies and crimes.

Planes Dropping Paratroopers Somewhere in Tennessee

Many soldiers from Camp Campbell learned about Middle Tennessee during World War II, when it was decided by the army that this area closely resembled where fighting was anticipated in the European theater.

Seven

In Harm's Way

IKE WITH PARATROOPERS

This postcard presents the same image as seen on the stamp on the card on the following page. Screaming Eagle faces are darkened with cork, cocoa, and cooking oil to prevent moon reflection. Drop sacks (with weapons) had been loaded aboard planes earlier. The photograph has been used as a standard for anything related to the European theatre of operations. Millions of reservists were called up in World War II. This photograph was taken on June 5, 1944, at Greenham Common Airfield at Newbury, England.

MAY OUR GLORIOUS FLAG AND THIS "LUCKY STAR"
GUIDE YOU AND KEEP YOU WHEREVER YOU ARE.

PATENT PENDING

This first-day cover of October 15, 1990, with the Dwight David Eisenhower stamp, shows him with 101st soldiers. At far right on the stamp image is William Crosby, of Reading, Massachusetts, a Jehovah's Witness who moved to the Florida Keys, where he died in the early 1980s. First Lt. Wallace C. Strobel, Easy Company, 502nd PIR, 101st, is jumpmaster for Aircraft #23—note the sign around his neck. Strobel died in Saginaw, Michigan, in 1999. Meticulous examination shows Screaming Eagles are smiling on the stamp but not in the image on the postcard.

"Swastika" comes from the Sanskrit *svastika* meaning "good," and the symbol has been used for more than 3,000 years. American Indians used it as a good luck symbol, and the 45th Division shoulder patch contained the symbol during World War I. Most modern societies associate the swastika with Hitler. There are five German POWs, captured in the Battle of North Africa, buried at Fort Campbell. The graves were at Lee Road and Bastogne Avenue but were relocated recently.

While Hitler was *Time's* coveted Man of the Year in 1938, history reveals him as a monster. The books that constitute the Hitler Library were discovered in a salt mine near Berchtesgaden haphazardly stashed in schnapps crates and then addressed for mailing by soldiers of the 101st in the spring of 1945. Hitler and his longtime mistress (then wife), Eva Braun, committed suicide on April 30, 1945.

This card was free-franked September 14, 1943, and passed by an army examiner when Pvt. Hayes Darrow mailed it to his mother in Ashland City, Tennessee. He wrote, "Just to let you know I am OK." On May 1, 1941, the first series-E savings bond was sold to President Roosevelt. By the end of World War II, over 85 million Americans had invested in savings bonds. Commodities were rationed, and Rosy the Riveter replaced the men turning out gas masks at Vulcan in Clarksville.

103

TROOP LADEN DUCK ON INVASION ROAD SO. FRANCE June 12, 1944

The 101st was here, as indicated in the Stars and Stripes booklet "All-American: The Story of the 82nd Airborne Division." This is near La Poterie, France. This card was a collaboration between the U.S. Army and General Motors. At the end of the war, the army was slashed from 8 million soldiers to less than 400,000. These boys were soldiers once, and young. Most are gone now.

Brig. Gen. Anthony MacAuliffe was commander of 101st at the Battle of the Bulge and saw fierce fighting. He was immortalized for a single word—"Nuts!"—which he exclaimed at the Germans' suggestion he surrender. He retired in 1956 and died in 1975. The main square in Bastogne is named for him, and this monument dedicated to him stands there. His son went to Armored Officer Candidate School at Fort Knox, Kentucky.

In 14 permanent European cemeteries, 93,103 American servicemen rest, while more than 110,400 originally buried in the region were returned home. Among those from Camp Campbell was 1st Lt. Thomas Meehan III, 506th PIR. His plane, loaded with Bangalore torpedoes, was hit by enemy fire and destroyed. All 21 aboard were killed. This cemetery is in Margraten, Holland.

Before Fort Campbell began deploying soldiers to fight, Anderson's News Agency in Clarksville made this 10-pack of postcards available. It was costly at a dime, but many were bought and mailed. The cards can still be found easily, but the envelope has not survived well.

The monochromatic use of yellow and green ink is unique in this comical card. Comical military cards provide a source for studying military lingo. Often, scatological phrases (T.S. and SOS), puns, double entendres, and sarcasm are used in this type of card. They contain captions such as "Victory has 100 fathers, and defeat is an orphan."

This army 280-mm atomic cannon delivered the seven-mile atomic projectile on May 25, 1953. It was a 15-kiloton detonation at the Frenchman Flat Nevada Test Site. Twenty 280-mm cannons were manufactured, but none were ever used in battle. In July 1945, the first atomic bomb was tested near Alamogordo, New Mexico, and in August, one was dropped on Hiroshima. The Manhattan Project resulted in the first and only nuclear bombs ever dropped in warfare. Shortly after they were dropped, the 101st deployed to Japan.

Check Point Charlie, going into the Eastern Sector of Berlin, was one of many checkpoints. Allied military members could not be checked at Friedrichstrasse or at the lesser-known checkpoints. The checkpoints and the wall all went away in 1989 and 1990. Many Fort Campbell soldiers do tours in Germany and often marry German girls.

The 1954 landmark Supreme Court decision striking down racial segregation in public schools opened the way for Little Rock's Central High School to be the first to integrate. In September 1957, President Eisenhower assigned the 101st to ensure that it was done peacefully.

The navy goes to Japan, the army to Korea. This is where we initially suffered the worst military beating in our history. Many young soldiers find Korean culture appealing, and around Fort Campbell, there is a sizeable Korean community.

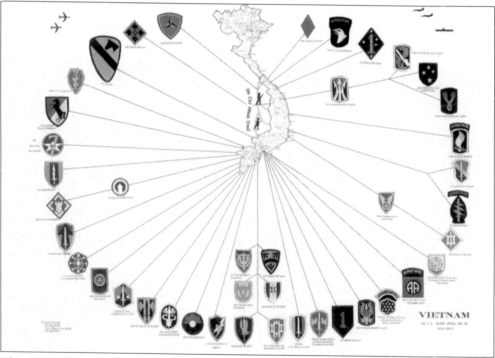

This postcard shows a map of Vietnam and unit patches showing the location of major units in 1968. Former 101st colonel David Hackworth authored *Steel My Soldiers' Heart's* about this horrific place after serving there with the 1st Brigade. The 101st accounted for 9,953 enemy killed as the scream of the eagle was heard all over Southeast Asia. Areas of operations were established in places no one could pronounce like Ap Bia, which we later nicknamed Hamburger Hill.

This card is "Courtesy of The Tidings, Los Angeles, October 7, 1966." Far too many Fort Campbell soldiers were killed in Vietnam, and this card demonstrates resentment for the Russians who provided support for "Charlie." In January 1973, Lt. Col. William Nolte was last American killed in Vietnam. Coming home from the war was not a pleasant experience for veterans who were spat on, called "baby-killers," and blamed for the misadventures of politicians.

The 101st participated in Operation Urgent Fury in 1983 in Grenada. Seven thousand U.S. troops, aided by 300 from neighboring islands, took on fewer than 2,200 rag-tag resisters. We lost 19 and they lost 102.

Service during Operation Desert Shield in the Persian Gulf gave the 101st yet another opportunity to prove themselves, and they did. The 101st soldiers who deployed here lived under austere conditions. The 5-101st served with distinction during Desert Shield and Desert Storm. They planned and led the world's largest air assault, which spearheaded the 101st Airborne Division's G-Day attack into Iraq.

Many new issues surfaced during this time. Single parents in the army were just one of them. The army granted Sgt. Nia Salakielu, a Clarksville woman, an exemption to recall and deployment because she "had no one to care for her child."

Chinook helicopters are a common sight around CAAF.

Aerial of The Pentagon   *Photo by J. Dunn*

At a cost of $83 million, the Pentagon enabled the consolidation of 17 War Department buildings. Located on 280 acres, including 67 acres of parking, the Pentagon was completed on January 15, 1943, and houses more than 23,000 people. Many Fort Campbell soldiers have served here.

Soldiers from the 101st killed Saddam Hussein's eldest sons, Uday and Qusai, in July 2003, and though the 4th Infantry captured Saddam, the 101st played a significant supportive role in his capture. The Screaming Eagle (depicted on this card) screams "Justice" with Saddam's capture. A number of 101st soldiers were killed in stepped-up attacks immediately after his capture.

The U.S. Armed Forces lost approximately three men per day during the first two years of Operation Iraqi Freedom. Sgt. Maj. Michael Stack of the 5th Special Forces Group, Fort Campbell, lost his life when his convoy was ambushed near Baghdad. There have also been several dozen Department of Defense (DOD) civilians killed. Many more Iraqis have been killed. Clarksvillian Michael Moseley, who was senior consultant to the Iraqi Ministry of Electricity, sent the author this card while he was working with DOD in Baghdad.

TASC artist Bob Goodwin did a number of prints of 101st soldiers in Vietnam. On January 23, 1973, a cease-fire was called there. At the same time, soldiers newly assigned to Fort Campbell, like Pvt. Troy L. Craig, HQ and Service Battalion, 101st Airborne Division Artillery, were working with portable field generators on a local field training exercise. They would not experience the feverish pace that had been the norm there for so many years.

AMERICA'S DARKEST MOMENT

Twin Towers always in our hearts   *New York, September 11ᵗʰ, 2001*

On that fateful day that would be known forever as simply "9-11," Fort Campbell rocketed into heightened alert status under the command of Maj. Gen. Dick Cody and closed the post except for Gate 4. A 100-percent ID check was instituted, deliveries were suspended, and armed guards were placed all around the post.

This is psychological operations (PSYOPs) at its finest. U.S. aircraft dropped these doctored bank notes in 1991. The backside identified them as Safe Conduct Passes and narrative translated to "You do not have to die. You can be Safe . . . follow these steps . . . hold your hands high in the air with this note showing and advance to American lines for surrender." There is also a mention of monetary reward. The 311th Military Intelligence Battalion is one of the Fort Campbell units engaged in psychological warfare in Iraq and Afghanistan.

While this card is funny, army families do find themselves in harm's way occasionally. The army goes to great lengths to get families out of areas that unexpectedly become volatile or hostile.

Eight

MISCELLANEOUS VIEWS

Fort Campbell's 11th Airborne commanders were: Maj. Gen. William M. Miley (January 1948–January 1950), Maj. Gen. Lyman L. Lemnitzer (January 1950–November 1951), Maj. Gen. Wayne C. Smith (November 1951–January 1952), Maj. Gen. Ridgely Gaither (January 1952–April 1953), Maj. Gen. Wayne C. Smith (May 1953–May 1955), Maj. Gen. Derrill McDaniel (June 1955–September 1956), Maj. Gen. Hugh P. Harris (October 1956–April 1958), and Maj. Gen. Ralph Cooper (May 1958–June 1958 [inactivated]). Shown here is an unidentified 11th Airborne soldier.

Steve Streck
15 S. Brill Ave.
Berlin, N. J. PO 207

KBV-7412 CH-18 ALL 23
JUMPER

Steve Streck of Berlin, New Jersey, may no longer be on active duty, but once a Screaming Eagle, always a Screaming Eagle. Amateur radio operators, to notify other operators that their transmission had been received, used QSL cards. "QSL" is the radiotelegraph code meaning "I confirm." It is neither an abbreviation nor an acronym. This was international Q-code acknowledgment of contact between two amateur radio stations.

Carlton & Walker Bousman - Rte 8, Clarksville, Tenn.
Ch: 11   KMM 8263   Ch: 9

Carlton Bousman was a lieutenant during World War II, owned Gate Three Printing, published the *Montgomery County News*, and was a relentless supporter of Fort Campbell, her soldiers, and the army. In 1989, the United States launched Operation Just Cause, sending troops into Panama to topple the government of Gen. Manuel Noriega. On January 3, 1990, Fort Campbell's Gen. "Smoking Joe" Kinzer (a fine officer and good soldier) penned a letter at Noriega's desk on Noriega's stationery and mailed it to Carlton.

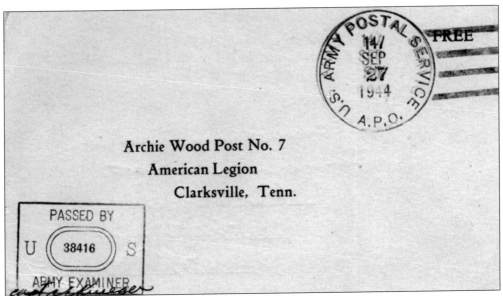

This card was free-franked and examined by the army during World War II. On the reverse, a soldier from Company B, 8th Tank Battalion, thanks American Legion Post Number Seven for sending him Chesterfield cigarettes.

This popular eatery on Murfreesboro Road, near Nashville International Airport, pays the 101st the highest compliment by using its name. The restaurant and its property are rich in wartime nostalgia.

CLARKSVILLE, TENN. and HOPKINSVILLE, KY.

Mrs. Jessie Milroy
213 S. William St.
Johnstown, N.Y.

Lt. John O. Thisler, public relations officer for Camp Campbell HQ, states in the folder that "First earth was broken in the building period January 26, 1942." On November 28, 1942, the first African American chaplain arrived to serve the thousands of black troops now stationed here. In 1943, units at the camp included the 1580th Service Unit at Post HQ, 1539th Service Unit, and Sub-School for Bakers and Cooks No. 4 of the 5th Service Command.

GREETINGS FROM CLARKSVILLE, TENN   CAMP CAMPBELL   11723

Mailed to Miss Margaret Goss of Pittsburg on February 13, 1943, this message declares, "Arrived safe, John sure looks nice in his uniform. Love Leola." The generic card is interesting because it implies Camp Campbell is in Clarksville, Tennessee.

GREETINGS FROM FORT CAMPBELL KENTUCKY

BETWEEN HOPKINSVILLE, KY., AND CLARKSVILLE, TENN.

These are referred to in postcard circles as "Large Letter Postcards." This large letter card includes an image of an antenna constructed by communications folks in the last letter. The views in each of the large letters are usually identified by narrative on the back of the card, and there are also individual cards of each scene. Country-and-western legend John Conlee shot the video for "They Also Serve" at Fort Campbell in November 2004.

Fort Campbell Kentucky

This postcard shows a drawing of a trooper of the 101st Airborne Division that parachuted into Normandy on D–Day in 1944. War has morphed from cannonballs to smart bombs and missiles, and while things are changing, the grunt is still the most important ingredient.

On July 5, 1999, 21-year-old Fort Campbell PFC Barry Winchell (perceived to be gay) was brutally murdered by fellow soldiers Calvin Glover and Spc. Justin R. Fisher. All three were in 2nd Battalion, 502nd Infantry Regiment. Democrats and the army Inspector General were not kind to Fort Campbell commander Maj. Gen. Robert Clark but exonerated him of accusations he encouraged a homophobic and disorderly atmosphere at the post.

These are two three-inch by four-and-a-half-inch match covers (a front view of one, the back of the other) that were often available in Camp Campbell service clubs. Once used, the matches could be removed and the inside of the cover had a place identified for a stamp, address and message. The "match cover postcard" could then be mailed.

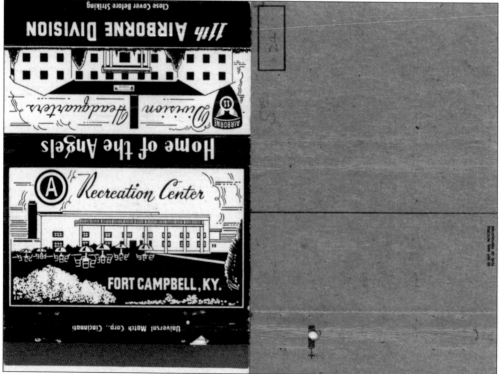

Members of Airborne Division at Fort Campbell, Ky. Bow their heads in prayer for former men who gave their lives during World War II

This is a memorial service, as described on the card. Three general-officer flags fly in the background. There is a message on the back of this card from the CG to newly assigned soldiers.

An A-10 Warthog (with its landing gear collapsed) is uglier than usual.

The 11th Airborne Division served with distinction and honor from November 1942 to July 1958. Comprised of former glider troops and veteran airborne troopers known as the "Angels," they killed 6,000 Japanese in the Philippines, many in hand-to-hand combat. In 1945, they escorted MacArthur into Japan and remained there until sent to Fort Campbell in 1949 as a training division.

Among those identified who greeted President Reagan in 1984 are, from left to right, Alfred Reeves (in white), who parked Air Force One; Maj. Gen. James E. Thompson; Hopkinsville mayor Sherrill L. Jeffers; and Clarksville's Ted Crozier. Other VIPs in attendance that day but not seen here were Brig. Gen. Gary Luck; Col. and Mrs. Robert Freeman; Col. Bruce Moore, commander 3rd Brigade; FAA representative Bill Duncan; CAAF commander Lieutenant Colonel Abbott; and Capt. Mike Clancy, commander 101st MP Company. The author was also there and shook hands and spoke with the commander-in-chief.

The fabled Stockade Annie (Anna Mabry Barr) cuts her 91st birthday cake as Maj. Gen. Olinto Mark Barsanti looks on. One of the last people to fight the government when families were displaced so Camp Campbell could be built, Annie became a true friend to Camp Campbell soldiers. She related especially to "the boys in the stockade," to whom she took Bibles. She was published under the pen name Garroway Renfrew.

Department of Army civilians Cathy Pierce (left) and Beverly Maki were deployed with units from the 101st to JRTC at Fort Polk. They wore battle-dress uniforms and drove their own HUMVEE. Many Fort Campbell soldiers knew Cathy (safety director) and Beverly (safety specialist)—they conducted safety inspections of deploying units, investigated serious accidents, and provided units with risk management training.

IN NEW YORK IT'S CHESTERFIELD *Joe Louis*
...the CHAMP of CIGARETTES

THE WINNER

Joe Louis fought exhibition fights at Fort Campbell during World War II while he was on active duty.

Marine Corps colonel Oliver North gained fame during the Iran Contra scandal. Later, as a conservative columnist, he would often write glowing things about the 101st.

Colonel Oliver North, armed with faith in God, love of country and the support of "my best friend"—his wife, Betsy, at the Joint House/Senate Committee.

The Bush family has been frequent visitors and great supporters of Fort Campbell. First Lady Barbara Bush is seen here with, from left to right, John Seymour, garrison commander; Seymour's wife, Mary; Maj. Gen. Bennie Peay's wife, Pam; Mrs. Bush; Mrs. Burba; and General Burba.

Fort Campbell vehicles and equipment shown here have been rail-loaded for a trip to Fort Chaffee, Arkansas. Soldiers are completing the process of tying the rolling stock down and ensuring all equipment is secure. This 1980s image includes a section of Fort Campbell's railroad.

As their birds lift off, young camouflaged soldiers look to each other for reassurance during training exercises at Fort Campbell.

Cherry Farm Limited, of 1237 Dover Road in Clarksville, created this card. The drawings are the work of artist Mike Ross, who also did political cartoons for *The Leaf-Chronicle*. These cards were printed in 1998.

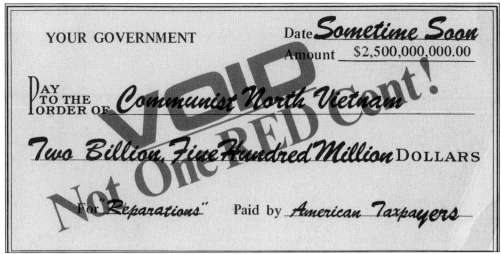

This is a postcard printed in 1973 by American Opinion opposing proposals to give $2.5 billion to help re-build Communist North Vietnam. It states that "such aid to an enemy that killed, maimed, and tortured thousands of Americans is outrageous." The card is addressed to CWO Michael Blaise, B Troop, 2nd Battalion, 17th Cavalry Regiment, 101st Aviation Brigade. The war influenced Nixon, and he ended military conscription, with the last draftees being inducted in December 1972.

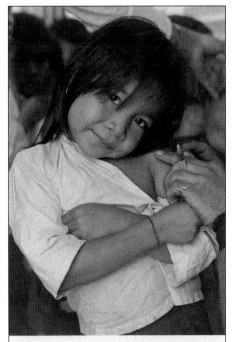

LY TRA, Vietnam—MODESTY. This pretty little lady presents a coy portrait as she receives her smallpox vaccination during a MEDCAP conducted by paratroopers of 1st Bn.(Abn), 327th Inf. here. Two-hundred and thirty children were inoculated against cholera and smallpox. (USA Photo by Spec. 4 Robert Chambers)

In Ly Tra, the army did wonderful things. My Lai was a different story. Many believe war makes it impossible to comply with the Geneva Convention guidelines.

Devada Elliot from the Palmyra area was married to Fort Campbell soldier William Stanley until they were sent to Germany and they met Elvis. Elvis's mother, Gladys, died, and Devada (right) divorced Stanley and married Elvis's father, Vernon (left).

Jay Leno and his wife, Mavis Nicholson (a writer), frolic with two soldiers from Fort Campbell during a visit to Iraq. With them are S1C Purdom, protocol NCOIC (non-commissioned officer in charge) and Capt. A. B. Cooper (now a lieutenant colonel). This was in 1990.